MAGICAL SECRETS OF THE CATICORNS

BY LIZ PALMIERI-COONLEY

Magical Secrets of the Caticorns

Copyright © 2020 by Liz Palmieri-Coonley

All rights reserved. No part of this publication may be reproduced, distributed, or transmitted, in any form or by any means, including photocopying, recording, or other electronic or mechanical methods, without the prior written permission of the publisher or author, except in the case of brief quotations embodied in critical reviews and certain other noncommercial uses permitted by copyright law. For information, contact Liz Palmieri-Coonley at www.AllThingsLizLoves.com.

ISBN 978-1-949142-06-8

Printed in the United States of America

MOST PEOPLE THINK THAT THE CATICORNS GET THEIR SECRET MAGIC FROM THEIR HORNS. THE REAL MAGIC COMES FROM THEIR WORDS.

EACH PAGE OF THIS BOOK SHARES A LITTLE MORE OF THEIR SECRET MAGIC. BE SURE TO READ THE MAGIC OUT LOUD AND TAKE THE CATICORN OATH AT THE END OF THE BOOK.

STAY MAGICAL,
LIZ

P.S. THIS BOOK IS DEDICATED TO MY SQUIDGEY BOO

EVERY PROBLEM HAS AN ANSWER

I CAN CONTROL MY OWN HAPPINESS

ANYTHING IS POSSIBLE

TODAY I WILL SPREAD POSITIVITY

MY VOICE MATTERS

I CAN CHANGE THE WORLD

I AM BEAUTIFUL INSIDE AND OUT

MY POSSIBILITIES ARE ENDLESS

TODAY I AM GOING TO SHINE

I AM GRATEFUL FOR ALL THAT I HAVE AND ALL THAT I AM

I AM STRONG AND DETERMINED

MONEY COMES TO ME EASILY

EVERY DAY I AM GETTING HEALTHIER AND STRONGER

GOOD THINGS ARE HAPPENING

I TELL THE TRUTH AND SPEAK FROM MY HEART

MY FEELINGS MATTER

I RESPECT PEOPLE THAT ARE DIFFERENT THAN ME

I PROTECT ALL LIVING CREATURES

I AM GOOD ENOUGH

I AM SURROUNDED BY LOVE

ABOUT THE AUTHOR

LIZ PALMIERI-COONLEY IS AN AUTHOR, 200-HOUR REGISTERED YOGA TEACHER, AND INTEGRATIVE NUTRITION HEALTH COACH. SHE IS ALSO A CERTIFIED KIDS YOGA TEACHER WITH KIDDING AROUND YOGA.

SHE GREW UP WITH A FASCINATION FOR THE HUMAN BODY, ILLNESS, AND HEALING, WHICH MAY SEEM WEIRD FOR A KID, BUT IT MAKES TOTAL SENSE CONSIDERING BOTH OF HER PARENTS WERE IN THE MEDICAL FIELD.

IN ADDITION TO HER LOVE FOR EDUCATING OTHERS ON YOGA AND HOLISTIC HEALTH, LIZ IS PASSIONATE ABOUT TRAVELING, SPENDING TIME OUTDOORS, AND EVERYTHING ABOUT HER INCREDIBLE NIECES. SOME OF HER MORE EPIC ADVENTURES INCLUDE: SCUBA DIVING, CLIMBING A WATERFALL, AND RIDING IN A HOT AIR BALLOON.

CATICORN OATH

I PROMISE TO READ THESE SECRET MAGIC WORDS OUT LOUD EVERY MORNING AND EVERY NIGHT.

I PROMISE TO SHARE THESE SECRET MAGIC WORDS WITH MY FAMILY AND FRIENDS.

I PROMISE TO MAKE EACH DAY AS MAGICAL AS POSSIBLE.